Gianni, Jan & Marcello Liscia

WORKBOOK EDUCATION

Personal and employee education

Illustrations:
Herman Reichold

Education is the third of five books in the D.R.E.A.M. of LEADERS®
publication series.

Bibliographic information of the The German National Library: The German National Library lists this publication in the German National Bibliography; detailed bibliographic data can be found on the website at http://dnb.dnb.de.

1ˢᵗ edition 2018

Imprint
© 2018 Gianni, Jan & Marcello Liscia

Layout, cover + worksheets: Franziska Eikel, Liscia Consulting
English translation by Ramey Rieger: doitwritetranslations@gmx.de

Text + Layout:
Biographiewerkstatt Böddeker
Ellerstraße 26 – 33100 Paderborn
Telephone: 05293 - 9327816

Print and publishers: : Books on Demand, Norderstedt
ISBN: 978-3-7528-5826-6

Table of Contents

"Learning is like rowing against the tide –
As soon as we stop, we drift back"[1]
Benjamin Britten (British composer, conductor and pianist)

Dear Reader,

Greetings and welcome to our *Workbook: Education*! Since you are holding our fourth book in your hands, you most likely already know our *D.R.E.A.M. of LEADERS®. Leadership is not an Illusion*, as well as our *Workbook: Dedication* and *Workbook: Responsibility*.

You don't? Then let us give you a brief introduction. For over 15 years, we at Liscia Consulting have been accompanying people along their paths to professional development. This is more than our career choice, it is our calling – the most amazing job we can imagine!

Our emphasis lays in advancing leaders, for which have developed the D.R.E.A.M. Formula[2], the essence of our years of experience:

D   Dedication: Wholehearted commitment to mission, 24 hours a day
R   Responsibility: Assuming full responsibility for your decisions, for your staff and for yourself
E   Education: Ensuring you and your staff evolve
A   Attitude: Living and communicating your personal mindset (philosophy) and values
M   Motivation: Commitment as the foundation of all deeds

The D.R.E.A.M. Formula acronym can also be understood as a checklist, illustrating the self-concept of a leader. It is how leadership can be understood and lived.

---

[1]   Unspecified quotes are taken from *Book of Quotations* (Bassermann-Verlag, 2013) or from digital quote collections.
[2]   D.R.E.A.M.-Formel® is a protected trademark owned by Liscia Consulting and registered with the German Patent and Trademark Office.

These are highly complex topics which we could not cover in differentiated detail in our first publication *D.R.E.A.M. of LEADERS®. Leadership is not an Illusion.* Hence, a separate workbook has been created for each letter in the D.R.E.A.M. Formula with which you can intensify and anchor your insights. Having read the preceding books is not necessary – each workbook is designed for independent use. The original chapters from *D.R.E.A.M. of LEADERS®. Leadership is not an Illusion* have retained their structure and been supplemented with additional examples for each letter. Worksheets at the end of each chapter allow you to practically apply knowledge gained.

We usually work with our clients over an extended time period, getting to know one another quite well. Our mission is people work, building relationships of equal standing, which is reflected in the language we use.[1]

This book provides in depth insight into the topic of education – what leaders can learn from star athletes, why strengths have a downside, what companies can do for their employees' growth, why horses are sometimes the best teachers, and more…

We wish you entertaining and edifying reading!

---

[1] To enhance readability, we have alternated masculine and feminine non-specific personal pronouns per chapter. Hence, in this context, we consider both genders gender-neutral and hope they are understood as such.

Education

CEO:	Imagine! Over the last 12 months, our leaders missed four whole days of work. They went to advanced training seminars.
LISCIA:	You don't say. What kind of seminar was it?
CEO:	Two days leadership training and two days training in each individual area.
LISCIA:	Let me get this straight. You say this was over the last 12 months. So, every 12 months you send each of your leaders to advanced training for four days?
CEO:	Are you serious?! What on earth for?
LISCIA:	Well, subtract four from about 230 workdays in a year, you've still got 226 days left.
CEO:	Mathematically, sure. But I'm not convinced. Still, I think I know where you're heading.
LISCIA:	Then let me map it out for you…

Of powerful leaders and outstanding athletes

A question we commonly ask leaders during our work together is, "When was the last time you worked on yourself? When was the last time you trained?"

The question doesn't refer to professional coaching or athletic training. The question refers to the last time the leader bought a book or journal on leadership. Or the last time she visited a trade fair. Not a branch-specific one, but a trade fair dealing solely with human resources and leadership. How long has it been since she spoke with a colleague about her employees, or sought a mentor?

These things are a part of advanced education. A leader must perpetually work on herself – that's what makes her a leader. It's not enough to undergo some training session simply because it's been a while since the last one, and the inner résumé update is looking rather thin. The basic message is non-stop improvement, honing and refining the most vital resource available to human beings – your brain.

Unfortunately, only a handful of managerial staff are aware of this. A favored analogy in this context is that of an outstanding athlete.

A dedicated sportswoman knows full well that she must consistently train six days a week in preparation for an hour of top performance on the weekend.

At the height of his career, Michael Schumacher drove up to 100 laps a day on the training track in Monza, Italy, striving to improve his performance at the next race by a mere tenth of a second.[1] The result of his training? Seven World Champion titles.

Recognizing this phenomenon, Canadian author and business advisor Malcolm Gladwell proposed the 10,000-Hour Rule. The rule implies that most geniuses, exceptional artists and highly successful entrepreneurs were not born magnificent, but amassed at least 10,000 hours of practice, culminating in their extraordinary performance, or even perfection, in their respective fields.

"Ericsson and colleagues (psychologists) then compared amateur pianists with professional pianists. The same pattern emerged. The amateurs never practiced more than about three hours a week throughout their childhood, and by the age of 20 they had totaled about two thousand hours of practice. The professionals, on the other hand, steadily increased their practice time every year, until by the age of 20 [...] they had reached ten thousand hours."[2]

And then there is Microsoft founder Bill Gates, one of the richest men in the world today, more than exemplifying the 10,000-Hour Rule. He began programing in the eighth grade, spending days and nights in the school computer room.

"By the time Bill Gates dropped out of Harvard after his sophomore year to try his hand at his own software company, he'd been programming practically non-stop for seven consecutive years. He was *way* past ten thousand hours."[3]

Managerial staff, however, seem to believe once they've finished professional school they no longer need to train or work on themselves. This is not only profoundly unprofessional - it's downright dilettantish. Professional leaders set the pace, not to mention the example, by working on themselves. They actively offer, or better, force advanced education opportunities onto their team and carry them out together. The only trustworthy and credible leader is one who walks what she talks.

But reality shows a very different picture. A survey of more than 10,000 employees throughout Germany, from a variety of sectors and company sizes revealed, "...that for their supervisors, further education played a minor role

---

[1]   Cf. Der Spiegel (41/2004), *Der spröde Held / The Aloof Hero*, pg.86 ff.

[2]   Gladwell, Malcolm, *Outliers. The Story of Success*, Bay Back Books 2009, pg.39

[3]   Ibid. pg.55

and there were few structured training programs offered in their companies[...] Thirty-nine percent of those surveyed are convinced their bosses don't even know which advanced training programs are available."[1] This is particularly baffling when you think about how digitalization has completely changed our working world. In nearly every field of business, employees continuously need updated training to keep pace with the ever-changing software, hardware and processing developments.

Aversity to advanced training seems to be a predominantly German phenomenon. Once Germans complete their studies or internship, they believe what they have learned is enough for their entire professional life. Furthermore, on the average, Germans only change jobs twice in their whole working life, whereas in the U.S.A., changing jobs more often is customary practice. U.S. Americans also frequently switch to a completely different sector or profession, a rare occurrence in Germany, and one that is more often than not frowned upon. And in your country?

We can see the advantages, however. By changing jobs, a worker is automatically compelled to adapt to a new situation, to absorb new knowledge. This is beneficial not only to the employer, but to the employee as well. Studies show that people who seek to increase their knowledge throughout their lives, remain mentally active much longer than those who do not. Learning also helps prevent diseases such as Alzheimer's.

When it comes to advanced education, companies are obligated to provide their employees with access to learning. An important catchword in this context is *knowledge management*. As we become increasingly aware of how significantly our employees' knowledge and skills contribute to economic success, these elements play an ever-stronger role in both strategic and operative leadership and personnel activities.

At the close of the 20th century, Dave Snowden, business advisor and knowledge management expert, developed the Cynefin Framework method. At the time, he was working for IBM, aiming toward creating a tool to better

---

[1] zeit.de, *Chefs interessieren sich zu wenig für betriebliche Bildung / Bosses display too little interest in company training*, 18.10.2016

manage the knowledge within his company. In the end, a tool emerged that went far beyond these humble aspirations. Cynefin Framework makes complex, incomprehensible coherencies graspable. The word *Cynefin* is Welsh, which can mean *habitat, rooted, acquainted, accustomed,* or *familiar* although the deeper sense of the term is lost in translation.

"Welsh scholar Dave Snowden chose the term to reflect the evolutionary nature of complex systems as well as their inherent contingencies. The name reminds us that all human interaction is powerfully influenced by our experiences; is most often determined by them – both our personal experience and the collective experience such as music or stories. The idea of the Cynefin framework is that it offers decision-makers a 'sense of place' from which to view their perceptions."[1]

Cynefin is composed of five domains or situations. The first domain is *disorder,* the condition of not-knowing which type of causality exists, making the situation impossible to grasp. This carries the risk of leaders withdrawing into their comfort zone when they are actually called on to make a decision. The objective is to gather as much information on the issue as possible and to distribute it among the four other domains.

The *simple domain* holds obvious problems with clearly denoted causes. Their solutions are evident, requiring a minimum of expertise and can be easily handled by non-qualified entities.

The *complicated domain* necessitates added expert knowledge. Here, the relationship between cause and effect is diffuse and must first be analyzed. You are aware of the cause, but it can have various effects. The complicated domain thus requires more time to clarify. Since the questions to be answered are known and there is some idea of the unknown, solution options are evolutionary, not revolutionary.

In the *complex domain,* there is neither an idea of the unknown nor are the questions to ask apparent. The effect is evident and definable, but the cause or causes are hidden from view. Thus, understanding the problem can only come about through trial and error. The path to solving the problem is unpredictable,

[1] https://de.wikipedia.org/wiki/Cynefin-Framework (German and English sites)

so the solution will only reveal itself when reached. In *complex* situations, new knowledge is primarily arrived at through experimentation, the results of which must first be evaluated before you can determine the next steps to take. Such situations call on your courage, curiosity and eagerness to experiment – aiming to make a *complex domain* a merely *complicated* one. You cannot premeditate or limit how much time this will take. As Thomas Alva Edison, U.S. American who invented the light bulb, put it in his famous quote, "I did not fail – I discovered 10,000 possibilities that didn't work."

Cynefin-Framework (Dave Snowden)

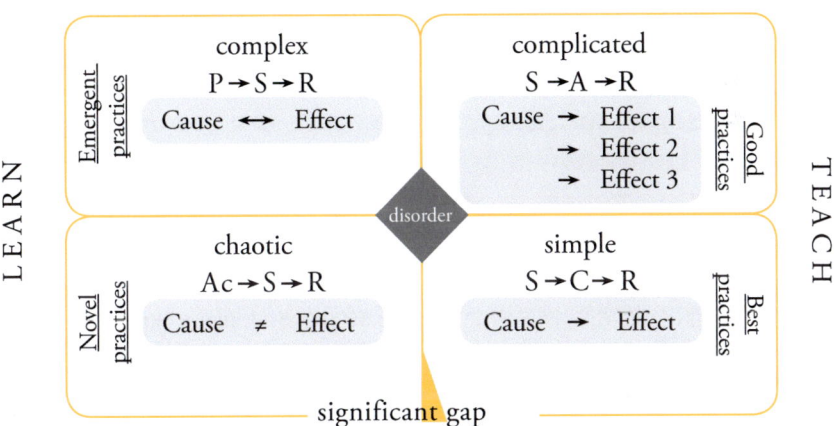

Cynefin = Welsh for habitat, rooted, situation

S = sense	R = respond	Ac = act
C = categorize	A = analyze	P = probe

In a *chaotic domain*, control has gone haywire and any rules there may be are lost in the maelstrom. People, machines and environment are at risk. Getting a grip on a *chaotic* situation is your top priority, seeking the simplest elements amid the chaos. Your goal is to instate partial results as quickly as humanly possible. As a leader, your role in a chaotic situation is to evince charisma and/ or dominance to reassure your employees and to avoid disruptive worry.

Over the years, the Cynefin Framework has become an efficient tool for knowledge management, change management, project management and group dynamics. Leaders must be prepared to adequately assess situations in order to react to them appropriately. Making a simple problem complicated only wastes your precious time. But, on the other hand, simplifying a complex domain can just as easily lead to chaos within your enterprise. The Cynefin Framework helps you categorize the manifold situations demanding decisions in your everyday professional dealings, providing you with concrete measures to initiate when addressing a given issue.

When broaching the topic of advanced education within your company, there are basically two approaches – skill management and competence management. Skill management addresses the knowledge your workers possess, that is which skills or abilities are needed to proficiently fulfill everyday tasks. This could be, for example, specific expert knowledge as stated in the employment announcement, i.e. programming languages, operating systems or linguistic skills, the latter categorized according to ability (basic knowledge, business confident, native speaker). In the Cynefin Framework, skill management is allocated into the *simple* and *complicated* domains.

In contrast, competence management is more a description of functions. It is the ability to transfer the qualifications, existing skills and knowledge onto precisely that situation where these specific attributes are currently needed. Therefore, competence management encompasses the entire Cynefin Framework, including the *complex* and *chaotic* domains.

Competence management is also directed toward autonomous learning – employees should absorb the competence necessary for their tasks first and foremost independently. This approach goes hand in hand with the *70:20:10* theory of learning, which has gained ground over the past years. The theory was developed by U.S. American scientist Morgan McCall with his colleagues Michael M. Lombardo and Robert W. Eichinger, who classified successful, efficient learning as follows.

Mastering everyday challenges at the workplace accounts for 70 percent of learning, i.e. learning by doing. Employee mentoring within the company, such as interaction with colleagues and superiors, supplies 20 percent of learning.

According to Morgan McCall, only 10 percent of learning is gained through external impulses such as training, seminars, coaching or e-learning.[1] Should this culture of learning become the norm, HR departments will have to completely rethink their employee development concepts, shifting their focus away from skill management and onto competence management.

Nonetheless, McCall's proposal that only 10 percent of learning ensues via external impulses should not be interpreted as a cost-savings rationale. *70:20:10* does not give companies license to cut back on advanced education investments, delegating the sole learning responsibility onto their employees. It is and will remain to be a company's obligation to give their workers access to the necessary advanced learning infrastructures. Should you take this obligation seriously, you must be willing to make initial investments – first *you* must support your staff if you expect to demand autonomous learning from *them* down the road.

Let's have a look at the 20 percent McCall allots for in-house mentoring. You must first establish the necessary structures within your company, it's not going to happen by itself. As a leader, you consciously decide to pass on your knowledge and so you acquire an education as in-house trainer, for example. In the chapter *Your employee's growth*, we introduce our *Business Trainer 2.0* program targeting employees of 55+ years – an efficient tool for businesses seeking to pass on their internal knowledge to as many of their employees as possible.

There's nothing new about this, by the way. Jack Welch, General Electric CEO from 1981 to 2001, coined the term *learning organization* as early as the 1980s, establishing an in-house Manager Academy.

"Strategy is unleashed when you have a learning organization where people thirst to do everything better every day. They draw on best practices from anywhere and push them to ever-higher levels of effectiveness. You can have the best big aha in the world, but without this learning culture in place, any sustainable competitive advantage will not last."[2]

---

[1] Cf. www.ccl.org/articles/leading-effectively-articles/the-70-20-10-rule and en.wikipedia.org/wiki/70/20/10_Model_(Learning_and_Development)

[2] http://www.karl-schlecht.de/fileadmin/daten/Download/Buecher/Welch-Winning-engl-orig.pdf

Due to digitalization and the technical options it provides, a *learning organization* has naturally evolved from its original concept in the 1980s. To create an environment conducive to autonomous learning, a company is also called on to invest in appropriate office renovations.

One current development is moving from open office concepts to the activity-based office.[1] The intention is to create retreat options where employees can concentrate on their work or on their learning – something which is impossible in open offices where the phone is constantly ringing, mails are coming in or colleagues are coming and going with various demands on my attention. My concentration is regularly interrupted, my stress level rises, and it can take up to eight minutes for me to refocus on the job at hand.[2]

In comparison, activity-based offices provide varying workplaces adapted to specific demands and to employees' actual needs. Each assignment category has its own space, thus, there are concentration, communication, collaboration and chill-out areas, to name a few.[3] When a worker retreats to the concentration area, he is not to be disturbed by anyone. Special wall lacquer prohibits cellphone reception.

To improve concentration, many companies no longer allow telephone conversations to take place at the desk. The moment the phone rings, a given employee dons a headset and retreats to a so-called cube – soundproof glass cubicles furnished with tables, chairs and technical equipment to access any necessary information. Here, telephone conversations are carried out comfortably without disturbing other co-workers.

Although such investments may be a financial challenge, the payback is worth it. Healthier work areas promoting concentration create space for effective, focused and engaged staff members, which, in turn, heightens their eagerness to learn and grow.

---

[1] Cf. youtube.com/watch?v=ipsWC3F2E-A

[2] Cf. welt.de, *Unterbrechungen treiben Stress auf die Spitze / Interruptions magnify stress*, 4.11.2013

[3] Cf. www.youtube.com/watch?v=UazUdUQn3s0

Key Lisciaman message
Just like star athletes, a leader must permanently train and work on herself. She must also give her employees access to learning. Failing to do so, she wastes valuable potential.

Your notes

Worksheet: Advancing yourself and your employees

Evolving as a leader

When was the last time you actively promoted your leadership development? What did you do, aside from reading this book right now (i.e. training, coaching, reading, trade fair – leadership-specific!)?

_____

_____

_____

_____

_____

_____

_____

_____

_____

_____

Make a list of all things you would like to do in the next 6 months to evolve as a leader!

_____

_____

_____

_____

_____

_____

_____

_____

_____

_____

Your employee's development

Now ask the same questions about your employees!
When and what did they most recently do for their development? Especially in relation to leadership development, when they have leading positions. When they have no leading role (and only then), in reference to their job-specific skills.

_____

_____

_____

_____

_____

_____

_____

_____

_____

_____

_____

_____

_____

Together with your employees, make a development wish-list for the next 6 months!

_____

_____

_____

_____

_____

_____

_____

_____

_____

_____

_____

Examine both wish-lists for their feasibility (financial, scheduling, organizational, etc.) and generate a plan to fulfil your and your employees' wishes!

CEO:	I was totally shocked to see how dismally Mr. Stone failed in leading the team! His career so far has been nothing short of amazing.
LISCIA:	You've never seen him fail before, have you?
CEO:	Never! He's my best man in the department.
LISCIA:	Then why did things go so wrong?
CEO:	I haven't the slightest idea. The best engineer is surely the best man to lead a team of engineers. That's obvious, isn't it?
LISCIA:	No.
CEO:	No?
LISCIA:	No.

The Peter Principle: Proximity Effect

Advanced training and qualification for employees plays a significant role in promotion. A competent leader takes pains to prepare the people entrusted to him for every new challenge.

A common fallacy when selecting a person for a new, more advanced assignment is basing the decision on his proficiency in his current responsibilities, and not on the attributes and insights he will bring to the future position. Overlooking this crucial distinction is known as the *proximity effect*, meaning the qualities of one criterion is transferred onto another, unrelated criterion.

This can have fatal repercussions. Just because someone does his line job exceedingly well, does not automatically mean he would make a suitable group leader. Nor would a good group leader necessarily make a good production coordinator – especially when he has not been given appropriate schooling beforehand. Promotion often entails giving an employee a higher position in the same area, increasing his or her responsibility. Without proper, specific preparation for the coming position, the candidate may soon be overwhelmed, which then has a myriad of negative impacts. Here, too, the leader is called on to assume full responsibility for his employees' quality of life.

(You will find more on the topic of a leaders' responsibility for employees' quality of life in our books *D.R.E.A.M. of LEADERS®. Leadership is not an Illusion* and *Workbook: Responsibility*.)

Every candidate for promotion should be carefully screened for the attributes and qualifications required for the future position. Otherwise, the problems will only multiply with each subsequent promotion. The U.S. American author Laurence J. Peter absorbed this insight and developed the *Peter Principle*.

Following the Peter Principle, every member in a sufficiently complex hierarchy is promoted until "they rise to their level of incompetence," meaning until they are in over their heads. This marks the end of his career advancement; he will no longer be promoted. Laurence J. Peter assumes "in time, every post (in a company, organization or civil office) tends to be occupied by an employee who is incompetent to carry out assigned duties."[1] A terrifying prospect that can only be countermanded by consistent qualification measures.

Apparently, prominent contemporaries are not immune to the proximity effect either. It was no surprise when reports of Germany's most successful tennis player, Boris Becker, and his financial difficulties made the rounds – it was well known that Becker was not a financial wizard. But when a London bankruptcy court announced his insolvency in June 2017, it was indeed a shock. After all, history's youngest Wimbledon victor had taken in 25 million euros in prize money alone, not to mention high-paying advertising contracts and TV appearances as well as his salary, earned training top athlete Novak Djokovic.[2] How could it be that someone so wealthy could not meet his financial obligations?

In the documentary *Boris Becker – Der Spieler / The Player*, which aired on German television in 2017, tennis historian Chris Bowers had his say. Although he did not explicitly mention it, his explanation of the German record-holding tennis player's financial malady is an outstanding depiction of the proximity effect.

"Becker's financial situation has long been an open secret in professional tennis circles. We knew he spent time in his London office, but no one knew what he actually did there. I don't wish to step on his toes, but it's possible he was not quite as successful a businessman as he was a tennis player. For some

---

[1]   Cf. Peter, Laurence J., Hull, Raymond, *The Peter Principle*, William Morrow and Company 1969

[2]   Cf. tagesspiegel.de, *Kann man mit 800.000 Euro im Jahr leben? / Is 800,000 euros enough to live on?*, 22.06.2017

reason, people always seem to believe if you excel at one thing, you automatically excel in other areas. But that is rarely true."[1]

This includes the realization that there are employees who essentially do not want to be promoted. It's quite possible to make a person profoundly unhappy by raising them to a post they never wanted – even if the money is more than good. Should this occur, all parties involved must have the courage to revoke the promotion, allowing the colleague to resume his preferred duties. This, of course is less than ideal, and it is a leader's duty to ensure it does not happen.

Felix, a production co-worker at a factory in the Ruhr Valley, Germany, whom we accompanied for quite some time, perfectly illustrates this. Felix works the line but is in truth a leader. He lives out his leadership qualities in his private life, as the leading elder of a New Apostolic congregation. His church responsibilities fully satisfy his inherent leadership drive.

Felix' superiors were ignorant of his off-time activities and urged him time and again to become team leader, an offer he repeatedly turned down. Having known him for many years, we, too, were attracted to Felix' talents and his consistently amiable demeanor. Felix was never disgruntled and was always ready to give a smile.

We were also convinced he would make an excellent team leader, so we invited him for a talk. He told us of his responsibilities in leading the congregation, and therefore simply wanted to work his shifts at the factory without taking on any added responsibility. This was only possible when he stayed on the production line. He was a highly reliable worker and assured us he enjoyed his work very much. We had always known that his engaging personality was an asset to the work environment.

After this talk, we explained to the bosses that they would have to accept Felix' decision to not become team leader and should no longer urge him to do so. Had they continued to pressure Felix, and he eventually capitulated, he would have eventually become a frustrated, dissatisfied employee. Why take the risk? His employer gains much more when he happily stands on the production line, motivating his colleagues with his steady good humor.

---

[1]   German TV: Das Erste, Boris Becker – *Der Spieler* / *The Player*, 20.11.2017. Paraphrased quote.

Key Lisciaman message
An employee doing an excellent job in his current position does not automatically qualify him for a higher position. As a leader, you must adequately prepare your employees for promotion to avert over-extension and failure.

Your notes

_____
_____
_____
_____
_____
_____
_____
_____
_____
_____
_____
_____
_____
_____
_____
_____

Worksheet: Observe your employees and yourself!

Looking back into the past, with which tasks or in which position could your co-workers have needed more support to be better equipped to fulfil their responsibilities?

_____
_____
_____
_____
_____

Now, in the current situation or looking ahead into the future, with which tasks or in which position do/will your co-workers need support, either from you or a third party? What shape does/will this support take?

_____
_____
_____
_____
_____

Which of your employees should you 'bail out' of a current task or position because she or he is overwhelmed and/or doesn't want to do/hold it in the first place? It could be that a one-on-one conversation is necessary before answering this question.

_____
_____
_____
_____
_____

Now, ask yourself the same questions, referring to your own tasks and position!

_____

_____

_____

_____

_____

_____

CEO:	Everyone can't just go around picking the cherries out of the cake!
LISCIA:	If you're a great fan of cherries but there's never any in the cake or a colleague gets to them before you do, that can be very frustrating.
CEO:	This is a company, not a kindergarten!
LISCIA:	You're the one who brought up the cherry cake.
CEO:	That was a metaphor. I like to talk in pictures.
LISCIA:	Yellow.
CEO:	What?

HBDI® – Strengthening strengths, weakening weaknesses

The scenario with Felix makes one thing perfectly clear, the better I know a person – in this case an employee – the better I can appreciate which tasks are best suited to her talents and abilities and which are not.

Having realized this many years ago, we acquired the license to implement HBDI®, a method of defining personality profiles. HBDI® stands for Herrmann Brain Dominance Instrument, the brainchild of Ned Herrmann, who developed the method in the eighties during his time as manager development director at General Electric.

HBDI® reveals an individual's or an entire team's preferred way of thinking; how these preferences change under stress, and how to mine untapped ways of thinking. It is one of the few scientifically validated methods in the field of personality profile building.

The HBDI® questionnaire is the first step to illustrating a person's way of thinking, also called the four facets of I. The resulting graphic model is divided into four quadrants, each of a distinct color. The rational-analytical I is blue; the practical-cautious I is green; relational-emphatic, red; and the experimental-intuitive, yellow. Every person has a uniquely configured combination of the four facets of I, therefore each quadrant is subdivided into four areas, i.e. avoidance, usage, preference, high preference. This precise differentiation allows a person to be described with profound accuracy.

Leaders, advisors or trainers truly mastering the HBDI® will certainly not know all facets of a personality once they have evaluated a candidate's questionnaire. What they will know is the singular configuration dominating the person's thought and speech. They will know which communication channels are most open to receiving and understanding a given message. These attributes make the HBDI® a highly efficient tool, especially in transitional processes. An employee whose preference lies in the green area – practical, cautious and security-oriented – will feel best in a familiar environment. She will most likely reject the prospect of change or be shocked by it. It is a leader's task to give her security.

And this security can be found by working with the *story changing®* board, for example. If the employee has already worked with this tool, she will feel a greater sense of security during the second transitional process. Her reliability, efficiency, sense of order and discipline in planning processes or carrying out projects are vital qualities upon which a leader can truly depend.

(You can read detailed information on *story changing®* in our books *D.R.E.A.M. of LEADERS®. Leadership is not an Illusion* and *Workbook: Responsibility.*)

A co-worker whose preference lies in the yellow area, will usually welcome change, as steady routines bore her to tears. Her restlessness can even cause her to leave the company, in search of new challenges. Her visual thought patterns enable her to surge forward, advancing innovative, original ideas and their realization.

The team member with blue preferences needs facts, numbers, statistics and factual data to satisfy her predominantly rational attributes. She is predestined to excel in financial, mathematical, analytical or technical areas.

On the other end of the scale, we find the employee with predominantly red thought patterns. This person has unhindered access to her emotions, cultivating communication skills and empathy with her fellow human beings. This predilection gives her the talent to train and teach others.

Now, your next logical question would be, "Is there an ideal profile for leaders?" The answer is, "No." You can lead from every dominant mode of thought. Most importantly, you must be just as aware of your weaknesses as you are of your strengths, applying the latter actively and intelligently to compensate for the former.

A powerful preference in one area is often perceived as strength. This, however is a much too one-sided interpretation, so allow us to clarify. On one hand, definitions such as *strength* or *weakness* have no significance for HBDI®– the focus is on categorizing preferred ways of thinking, as we initially explained, into the four areas – avoidance, usage, preference, high preference. On the other hand, a high preference may not be beneficial in all situations. It may well be that I occupy myself much too much with my preferred tasks, thereby neglecting others.

This is only natural. You would much rather spend time with something that lets you shine, than with something that makes you sweat. But you then run the risk of investing more time in these tasks than necessary. Imagine someone with a high preference in the green quadrant – someone systematic, structured, standardized and security-oriented. If allowed, this person would become thoroughly absorbed in tidying up, sorting, double-checking and pre-pre-preparing, just to be sure nothing has been overlooked. She would go completely overboard.

Initially, these processes would gratify her, this is where she shines. But there's a fine line between conscientiousness and compulsion. Thus, the high preference becomes a burden to her immediate surroundings. And in extreme cases, stress for the woman herself as her pedantic methodology leaves her little time and energy for other tasks. Here we can see how a high preference can indeed become a weakness. A weakness I must be aware of to better counteract it.

The same applies to the avoidance area. Once the HBDI®analysis has revealed this preference, I must develop a strategy to handle it appropriately. Completely circumventing avoidance areas is not possible, even though that may be our tendency. We must keep in mind that avoidance does not mean *I can't*, it really means *I won't*. There will always be situations demanding exactly those skills I don't possess. One solution could be to delegate such tasks, but if that's not possible I have to find a way to do it myself – without my avoidance areas adding to the burden each time.

In this case, support can be found in training or coaching, helping you find a practicable modus vivendi. Our seminar participants are often astonished when they discover that applying the appropriate tool actually does allow them to ably master avoidance area tasks. Here, the GROW coaching model, for example, would be applicable.

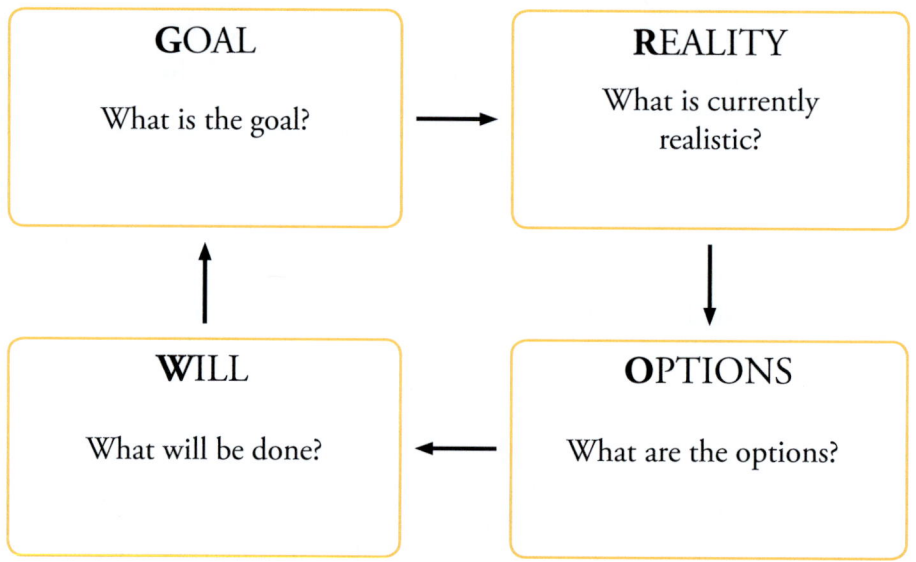

The first step of the GROW model broaches your *goal*. What is your objective in consciously confronting your avoidance area? Here's an example: One of our clients had installed a new project management software. The software is used to generate a uniform procedure for systemizing and structuring information. As a result, company transparency and knowledge management are enhanced by a compilation of information in one place, instead of in employees' heads or jotted down on a notepad somewhere. One of the executives had massive resistance to using the software – but not because he couldn't. Being a person with high creative and experimental preferences, while embodying avoidance of structures and organization at the same time, it wasn't as if he lacked the brainpower to master the software. His difficulty lay in the fact that it *just wasn't any fun*. But what is the goal? To transfer information from his head and notepad onto the system.

This brings us R as in *Reality*. What is the current situation, realistically?

Will this leader become an expert in the new system? Certainly not. But it is realistic for him to learn to work with the software. So, which *Options* do we have? One option would be for the executive to pass on his notes and thoughts to his assistant, either in written form or dictated to an audio file, having her write them up and enter them into the system. Another option would be that he learned the basics of working with the new system, enabling him to access information when he needed it.

The path from O for *Option* leads to W for *Will*. Which solutions were implemented; which ones worked? In this case, the leader sent audio files with information and assignments to his assistant who then accurately transposed them for the project management software. In addition, our client learned to work with the system well enough to access stored information.

This specific type of training can also lead to an avoidance area becoming a usage area – particularly when the preferences avoidance and usage are close neighbors. Here, we think of a plant manager at a large German media business. For years, he had refused to take part in the English classes provided by his employer. His reason being he simply did not have a talent for languages. This often gave rise to uncomfortable situations. Even though he worked solely on the German market, there is simply no getting around using English when working on the media sector. Nonetheless, he kept a firm grip on his resistance, "I am not going to take English lessons!"

One day, an attractive position opened up at his company's British subsidiary. A position tailored to his profile. His employer let him know he was the first choice for the job, but without the appropriate language skills, he didn't have a prayer. And what did the plant manager do? To the amazement of his superiors and colleagues he began participating in English lessons! Within six months he was business confident! Not that he suddenly acquired a liking for the English language. He simply wanted the alluring position in England, come hell or high water, and learning English was the only option. Hence, the motivation behind avoidance does not necessarily imply a lack of skills. It can simply imply an aversion to confronting certain tasks.

Here's a classic example – calculating travel expenses, an issue in many companies, ours included. Even though there's the reimbursement to look forward to, for most of us it's a yawning abyss to be crossed. Merely thinking of *supplementary catering expenditures* flat rate is enough to start rummaging around for an aspirin.

We have discovered that there are two approaches to the beast. Some take the bull by the horns and submit their calculations once a month, quick and simple. Others put it off until the end of the year, spending four or five days wrangling with receipts. Does this imply that the latter group is incompetent in this area? Not in the least. They simply ignore it until the end of the year, when it cannot be ignored any longer and must be done *now*.

This is related to the law of polarity, which we addressed in detail in our books *D.R.E.A.M. of LEADERS®. Leadership is not an Illusion* and *Workbook: Responsibility*. In short, the law of polarity asserts that everything I do or decide has its antithesis. You will find polarity everywhere, as it is how we perceive our world, by differentiating between two poles – good/evil; wrong/right; hot/cold; poor/rich; strengths/weaknesses, etc. With every *yes* I utter, I imply its counterpart, *no*.

In reference to our travel expense example, you could say that the second group follows this inner dictum, "I know I've put off calculating my niggling supplementary catering expenditures flat rate until the last minute, which probably means I'll have to forego joining my colleagues at the traditional Christmas Market in December, but I'm really late so it's now or never." They've avoided doing it an entire year, but that doesn't mean they *can't* do it, it means they *didn't want* to do it.

Understanding thought pattern preferences opens new awareness of your employees' potentials, while building an inimitable foundation for internal communications. You can only play to your employees' strengths when you know just what they are.

Ignoring your employees' qualities and potentials can cause you to place someone in a position contrary to her thought pattern preference, which leads not only to a dissatisfied colleague, but can also have a long-term negative impact on her engagement and efficiency.

Key Lisciaman message
The better a leader knows her workers, the more realistically she can evaluate which position suits them best. The HBDI® personality profile analysis opens new avenues of understanding your employees' potential.

Your notes

Worksheet: Examine the distribution of assignments among you and your team!

How would you characterize yourself and your employees/colleagues?
How would you allocate your peoples' traits among the four preferences? Note:
The same name can appear in two, three or all four preferences. The more often a name appears, the more likely this person is a jack of all trades; the more seldom, a specialist.

A: rational, analytical, logical, technical, mathematic, critical

_____

_____

_____

_____

B: security-dependent, structured, meticulous, sequential, organized

_____

_____

_____

_____

C: emotional, empathetic, interpersonal, harmony-dependent, communicative

_____

_____

_____

_____

D: experimental, intuitive, flexible, spontaneous, visual, creative

_____

_____

_____

_____

Use the same scheme to assess the tasks carried out by your team or department!

A: rational, analytical, logical, technical, mathematic, critical

_____

_____

_____

_____

B: security-dependent, structured, meticulous, sequential, organized

_____

_____

_____

_____

C: emotional, empathetic, interpersonal, harmony-dependent, communicative

_____

_____

_____

_____

D: experimental, intuitive, flexible, spontaneous, visual, creative

_____

_____

_____

_____

Now, compare your preferences and those of your employees. Which tasks are allocated according to preference? Which task distribution should you reconsider?

> CEO: We're not obligated to provide advanced training, that's the workers responsibility.
>
> LISCIA: So, you're saying, if you don't ask for it, you won't get it?
>
> CEO: Exactly. A person must know himself where his deficits lie.
>
> LISCIA: That only works when he's aware of his deficits. What if he's unaware of his incompetence?
>
> CEO: What do you mean by unaware?
>
> LISCIA: Why didn't you ask that before I used the word?
>
> CEO: I didn't know you were going to use it!
>
> LISCIA: My point exactly!

Your employees' growth

Once an employee is positioned in accordance with his thought preference, he can concentrate the entirety of his energies on his strengths, propelling his professional career forward. Companies are well-advised to actively support their employees' growth. It is a far better thing to invest time and energy in discovering the talents slumbering within your own ranks; to awaken them with well-aimed schooling and/or advanced training – than to waste time wailing about the shortage of skilled workers.[1]

In this context, we offer three programs. The first is a leader development program targeting employees who already hold management positions or are current candidates for the same. These do not necessarily have to be persons with leadership responsibilities, but they commonly are. The program not only provides general training sessions and workshops. It also entails individual coaching to specifically probe into the candidate's personal needs.

Our program for junior employees is much more comprehensive and aimed toward co-workers under 40 years of age. This program is not necessarily preparation for a leadership position, it also is geared toward specialists, another career option within a given company and a differentiated avenue of advancement that we profoundly advocate. Many companies are so focused on

---

[1] Cf. wiwo.de, *Unternehmen sind schuld am Fachkräftemangel / Businesses Invoke the Skilled Worker Shortage*, 13.10.2014

junior leaders that fostering specialists falls by the wayside. A dreadful waste.

So much talent is lost because not every established specialist is meant for leadership. Yet, a person not willing or able to become a leader has little chance of advancement and will therefore mostly likely abandon the enterprise.

Which is why business administration professor Benedikt Hackl at the Baden-Württemberg University also urges, "... in general, companies should offer a variety of career paths, 'Most people aspire to a leadership position simply for the higher salary. A business thereby loses their best specialists and gains the worst leaders.' Hackl advocates project and specialist careers that are as well-paid as leadership positions."[1]

In the first year of our program for junior employees, all participants undertake and complete a broad spectrum of training sessions and workshops. Deciding which path to take in the second year, leadership or specialist training, ensues during consultation with direct superiors.

We are currently carrying out this program at an industrial enterprise, schooling 37 employees. At the beginning of the second year, it looked as if 21 participants would take the leadership career path, undergoing a ten-day leadership training. The other 16 participants chose the specialist career path and will take part in a ten-day Train the Trainer course. In the end, being an expert is not enough. A specialist should also be capable of communicating with his environment and of passing his knowledge on to others.

Our third program is called Business Trainer 2.0 and is primarily tailored to employees of the 55+ generation. In essence, Train the Trainer is a promising channel for companies wishing to share their own knowledge and experience with as many employees as possible. In-house trainers become heralds of knowledge, which is immeasurably valuable to employers.

In view of the increasingly higher pension age, Business Trainer 2.0 serves the older generation well. As Senior Trainers, they bring added value to everyone involved. They not only motivate and bond with trainees, productively applying profound experience, they also safeguard hard-earned insights for the company's sole benefit. A Senior Trainer is also well-suited to optimizing interfaces by

---

[1] sueddeutsche.de, *Chefs, die nicht loslassen und Mitarbeiter, die nicht ranwollen / Leaders who won't let go and employees who don't want to lead*, 25.10.2016

skillfully guiding customers and suppliers, saving both time and money. The 2.0 category tag on this program implies the latest business method developments. It reflects our conviction that nowadays a senior Business Trainer will need to use new media. This not only includes top proficiency with Power Point but covers the spectrum from distributing tablets among trainees for document storage to applying e-learning tools. In addition, creating private groups on social media, such as LinkedIn, Yammer or Facebook, is excellent for giving participants a place to voice their opinions and exchange ideas. And every Business Trainer should know how to handle a drop box.

We see absolutely no contradiction between 2.0 and 55+, as it is precisely Millennials and Generation Z who will benefit from a Senior Trainer. Once candidates have completed our training, which also encompasses methodology and educational aspects, your experienced employees will own the skills to ably pass their knowledge onto the younger generation. It is vital however in this context to be aware of the varying approaches each generation takes to advanced education. In our books *D.R.E.A.M. of LEADERS®. Leadership is not an Illusion* and *Workbook: Attitude* we have talked about the challenges a leader faces when leading a team composed of four generations simultaneously. There is nothing exotic about teams made up of Baby Boomers (1945 – 1964), Generation X (mid-1960s to early 1980s), Millennials (Generation Y, early 1980s to early 2000), and Generation Z (mid-2000 to today), with each generation bringing their own values, perspectives and expectations. The same diversity applies to approaches to advanced education. While Baby Boomers are only moderately interested in further education, Generation X consider it a necessity. Millennials expect *continuing* advanced education; Gen Z assumes *permanent* advanced education is a given.

And then there is the varying learning styles. Baby Boomers absorb new knowledge via training sessions or seminars, while Generation X learns independently. This changes markedly with Millennials, the first digital natives, whose preferred learning style is team-oriented networking, while Gen Z learns almost exclusively using technology. For the latter, digital media is taken for granted, as Christian Schuldt of the *Zunkunftsinstitut / Institute of the Future* in Frankfurt am Main, Germany expresses it.

"Generation Y [...] clearly diverge from Gen Z in this respect. 'Generation Z was born into a mobile, internet world. They no longer adhere to the mobile-first doctrine, their credo is mobile only,' says Schuldt. The fast-draw cellphone is permanently loaded, and the world is experienced online."[1]

This has an impact on concentration, an important aspect of advanced education.

"Youth researcher Hurrelmann identified a new strength-weakness profile for the employees of tomorrow. 'We can expect a highly sensitized young generation, absorbing and grasping with lightning speed and extremely adept at multi-tasking,' he says, 'but they are less focused, easily distracted and with a low stamina level."[2]

Companies will have to adapt, holding appropriate learning options shaped to serve the pertinent generation. If they don't, they run the risk of losing valuable talents currently in their employ, who sooner or later will seek more attractive shores. With the growing shortage of skilled workers, a time will come when employers will apply to young workers for their services, instead of the other way around. Generation Z seeks security and predictability, making it quite feasible that they would commit to a single employer for a long time – possible their entire professional life.[3] But this generation is also highly self-confident and will not hesitate to change employers if personal growth and learning culture are not tailored to their needs.

When, as so often the case is, growth and development are the focus of our coaching, we like to apply Schulz von Thun's Value and Development Square, a method that he put back on the map and applied it in coaching and communication training, but is actually derived from Aristotle's *Virtue is the Golden Mean*, as developed by Paul Helwig (1893-1963) and Nicolai Hartmann (1882-1950).[4] Since we believe a model is only as good as its practical

[1] welt.de, *Was Generation Z vom Berufsleben erwartet / Gen Z's Career Demands*, 06.03.2016

[2] Ibid.

[3] donaukurier.de, *Die Jugend steuert der Zukunft entgegen. Audi veröffentlicht Studie zur "Generation Z" / Youth moving toward the future. Audi publishes a study on Generation Z*, 28.6.2017

[4] Cf. http://selbstlernkurse.forumzfd-akademie.de/valuesquare/01 (Translator's note: this site requires registration to access it)

application, we would like to describe the Value and Development Square from its theoretical outcome. Which, in the coaching process, is its practical launching pad, i.e. the identification of a behavioral habit that the coachee aims to kick, or more precisely, aims to bring into balance.

Let us illustrate this process with Damian. Damian came to us for coaching when a 360° feedback revealed an overabundance of authoritativeness and dominance in his leadership style. One feedback comment went so far as to clearly put forward that Damian "ruthlessly exercised his power." At first, Damian could not wholly identify with the epithet, but he was aware of how his colleagues and employees could come to such a conclusion. He also knew he had to work on his leadership style; to learn to open up and make more space for his employees' input. That they wished he would show more consideration was another issue on his roster.

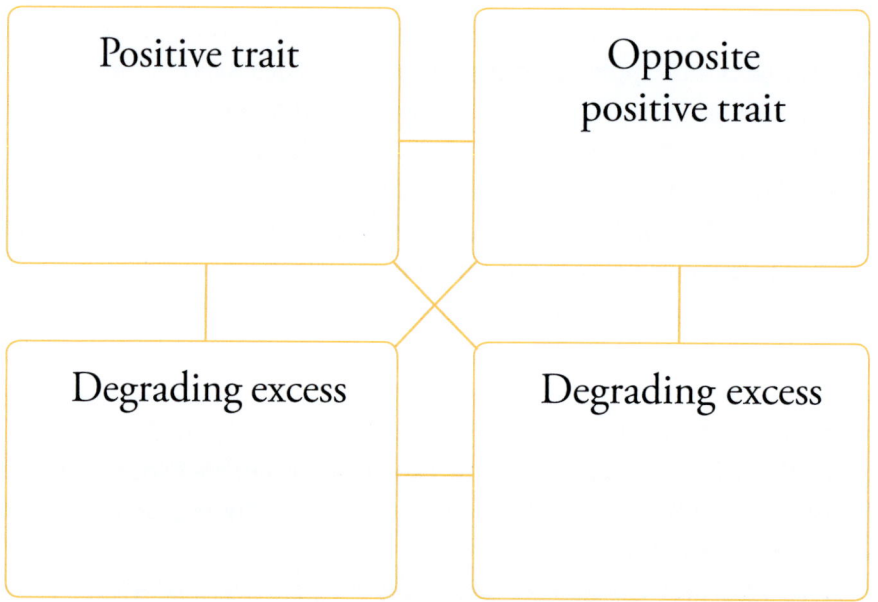

After reflecting on several recent situations, Damian was forced to swallow the bitter truth – he *did* exercise his power ruthlessly. This is the moment where we write down exactly these words on the lower left-hand corner of a piece of paper or on a whiteboard. As you can see in the figure, the lower left field denotes a degrading excess. In its essence, this *degrading excess* has its origin in a positive value that is generally accepted as something desirable. Together with Damian, we agreed to call this value *self-assertiveness*, a trait that – when not too pronounced – has altogether positive connotations. Now, as the model unfolds step by step, this *positive trait* is written in the upper left-hand corner, above the *degrading excess* value. This field in the model represents the original intention from which Damian's ruthless power-play most likely arose. You could also say that a return to this value and its corresponding behavior is the path Damian should take.

So far, so good, but not the whole model by a long shot. What's missing is an additional development path and a prospective confrontation, both found on the flip side of the coin, figuratively speaking. Practically speaking, these are found on the other side of the model, the right-hand side. The development path is best followed when you seek together the *opposite positive trait* to the one on the upper left-hand side. This should be a value that is commonly acknowledged. The opposite of self-assertiveness could easily be *consideration*. We intentionally use a subjunctive verb here as it is important that these values are sought together with the coachee. In a comparable situation with a different person, most likely other terms would be used, hence other values discovered.

For Damian, the development path was clear – to be more considerate of his employees' needs. And not only of them. Damian also recognized this interplay of values in his non-professional relationships. A more considerate behavior would help him to break away from his ruthlessness, to develop in an acceptable direction without relinquishing his original, native self-assertiveness.

To complete the model and give Damian food for thought as to how this degrading excess possibly came about, we work with the remaining field in the square on the lower right-hand corner. This field is both the opposite of the *confrontation area* (in Damian's case, ruthlessly exercising power) as well as the *degrading excess* of the upper right *opposite positive trait* (here, consideration). This can reflect the origin of a degrading excessive behavior, which *could* have been an exaggerated counterreaction to something a person wants to avoid at all costs, as this something is terrifying.

With Damian, we filled in the lower right confrontation area with the *degrading excesses* docility and self-denial. Damian recognized the role these two values had played in his youth and his conscious decision to develop in the opposing direction. He didn't want to go into detail, and there was absolutely no need for him to do so. The 360° feedback and coaching helped him to identify this mechanism and to set out in a new, positive direction, learning and growing along the way.

Key Lisciaman message
In these times of skilled work shortages,
companies require fine-tuned measures
to foster their employees' growth.
Only thusly, can they ensure the
enduring loyalty of their talented
employees.

Your notes

Worksheet: Applying the Value and Development Square

Apply the Value and Development Square to you and your employees! You can write your answers directly in the diagram on the following page.

1. Which degrading excess do you perceive in yourself/your employees? (lower left)

_____

_____

_____

_____

_____

2. Where does it come to a confrontation? (with situations, with persons, with yourself) (lower left)

_____

_____

_____

_____

_____

3. From which positive trait did the degrading excess emerge? (upper left)

_____

_____

_____

_____

_____

4. Which opposite positive trait do you perceive as development area? (upper right)

_____

_____

_____

_____

5. Which counteractive degrading excess emerges from question 1? (lower right)

_____

_____

_____

_____

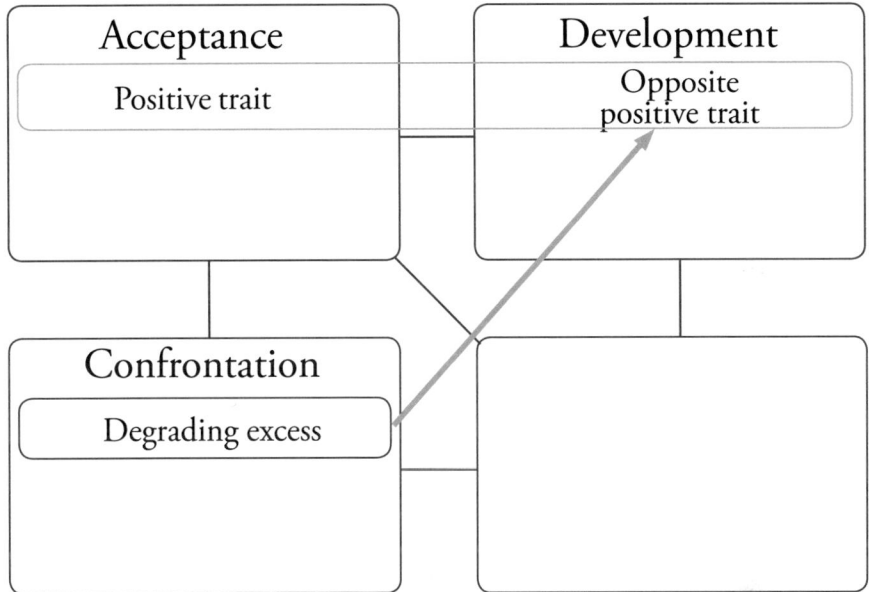

CEO:	Is that something like the seal principle, but without the seals?
LISCIA:	You must mean penguins.
CEO:	Why penguins?
LISCIA:	The principle you're talking about comes from penguins. But no, that's not what this is about. These are real horses.
CEO:	And the horses are observed?
LISCIA:	If anyone is observed, it's you – with the horse.
CEO:	I've never been on a horse before.
LISCIA:	That's even better!

Horse-assisted Coaching

There are times when you need to move in a completely new direction to gain fresh insights. Thus, we offer you horse-assisted coaching. Our co-worker Franziska - all-round office talent as well as graphics & design professional - is also an experienced horse trainer applying Monty Roberts' renowned Horse Whisperer methods. Franziska is our team's specialist in horse-assisted coaching, which primarily addresses your leader's social skills. While professional expertise is understandably indispensable, the value of social skills is very often depreciated. A good leader is proficient in both areas, applying and combining them according to the given situation.

Equine assisted coaching has nothing to do with horse-back riding. It is, among other things, learning to lead a horse through an arena – first with a lead line, then without. Will the horse have enough trust in its leader to accept her authority, following her the second time, without being physically led? Is the relationship strong enough, the trust solid enough, to keep the horse from shying away from unexpected events, such as walking over a crackling foil? If trust and authority falter, the horse will balk and refuse to go any further. A highly illuminating experience.

In equine assisted coaching, a leader's behavior is mirrored openly and honestly – a rare experience in professional life, especially for upper-story employees climbing the corporate ladder. Interacting with a horse gives a leader the singular opportunity to directly experience her impact on others.

She becomes sensitized to the subtlest signals in her own behavior, thereby schooling an authentic presence.

The results of equine assisted coaching are professionally analyzed and probed in a follow-up session. Which lead lines do I use in my team? Do I send clear signals? Do my employees trust me enough to follow me, even when the going gets tough? In this talk, the leader receives efficiently practicable suggestions to integrate into her everyday professional life.

Such was Frank's experience. Frank, one of three business executives at a software development firm, booked, along with his two colleagues, horse-assisted coaching with us. At the indoor riding arena, all three men were given a lead line. The horse trainer gave them their first task, which was to lead the horse, Jack, over the course without pulling on the lead line, i.e. keeping it loose in their hands. The course consisted of several pylons to lead the horse around as well as a crackling foil on the ground, over which the horse is to be led. His colleagues mastered the course without a hitch, but Jack refused Frank's leadership, even when he pulled on the lead line. The second part of the coaching is to lead the horse over the course again, this time without the lead line, yet leading all the same. As you might have guessed, Frank failed across the board.

Frank was stumped. What was he missing? What did his colleagues have that he didn't have? Later, as we watched the video recording, there was no doubt about it. Both of Frank's colleagues had approached Jack from the front, drawing Jack's full attention and affinity. Frank, on the other hand, had approached Jack from the rear, and as he did not once establish eye contact, Jack felt no obligation to acknowledge his existence. Not even when Frank pulled on the lead line. Furthermore, Frank failed to give Jack clear signals as what he was to do. Frank quickly ran through various methods – verbal and non-verbal – to get Jack to move.

Equipped with this knowledge, Frank gave it another go, first with the lead line, then without. This time he approached Jack frontally and immediately looked him in the eye. He was much calmer this time around and gave the horse clear signals. It worked!

We then analyzed together what these insights could mean for Frank's everyday professional life. How clearly did Frank communicate with his employees? Frank thought a moment. "There was a certain situation at the office last Monday," he related. "I went out to the front room where our two assistants work and asked if I could have the minutes of our last meeting. Both answered at once, 'Yes! Of course!' It would have been better to address just one of them by name, looking her in the eye, to make perfectly clear whom I meant." Frank also recalled other incidents that reflected his insubstantial communication and/or body language. On several occasions, he had noticed a rather testy atmosphere in the front room but had put it down to tension between the two workers and had nothing to do with him personally.

A few days later, Frank contacted us. He reported he had spoken with his assistants and they confirmed that Frank's vagueness about who should do what or exactly what was to be done frequently gave rise to tension between the two of them. They often had to bat the task back and forth to determine just who was going to do his bidding. Although they were both very dedicated employees, neither wanted to take on more work than was necessary.

Frank was relieved – without the horse-assisted coaching he would not have realized how murky his communication had been. He also recognized the same behavior when dealing with colleagues, superiors or customers, failing to find the optimal way to address them. He was determined to make his purpose more clear-cut in the future, avoiding misunderstandings all around.

Key Lisciaman message
Horse-assisted coaching reveals new insights into your leadership communication skills. An authentic presence is often a matter of subtle nuances, which the horse perceives and reflects back to you honestly and directly.

Your notes

_____

_____

_____

_____

_____

_____

_____

_____

_____

_____

_____

_____

_____

_____

_____

_____

_____

Worksheet: Your leadership behavior

How do you assess your demeanor and communication when dealing with your employees? What impression do you make? If you do not have leadership responsibilities, reflect on how you approach others in general!

Referring to the following attributes, evaluate your comportment on a scale from 1 to 10 (1 = not in the least; 10 = absolutely). Complete the list with attributes of your own!

convinced	1	2	3	4	5	6	7	8	9	10
convincing	1	2	3	4	5	6	7	8	9	10
credible	1	2	3	4	5	6	7	8	9	10
appreciative	1	2	3	4	5	6	7	8	9	10
respectful	1	2	3	4	5	6	7	8	9	10
trustworthy	1	2	3	4	5	6	7	8	9	10
clear	1	2	3	4	5	6	7	8	9	10
muddled	1	2	3	4	5	6	7	8	9	10
focused	1	2	3	4	5	6	7	8	9	10
authentic, integral	1	2	3	4	5	6	7	8	9	10
critical	1	2	3	4	5	6	7	8	9	10
authoritative	1	2	3	4	5	6	7	8	9	10
ruthless	1	2	3	4	5	6	7	8	9	10
dominant	1	2	3	4	5	6	7	8	9	10
unintelligible	1	2	3	4	5	6	7	8	9	10
ambiguous	1	2	3	4	5	6	7	8	9	10
....	1	2	3	4	5	6	7	8	9	10
....	1	2	3	4	5	6	7	8	9	10
....	1	2	3	4	5	6	7	8	9	10
....	1	2	3	4	5	6	7	8	9	10
....	1	2	3	4	5	6	7	8	9	10
....	1	2	3	4	5	6	7	8	9	10
....	1	2	3	4	5	6	7	8	9	10

	1	2	3	4	5	6	7	8	9	10
....	1	2	3	4	5	6	7	8	9	10
....	1	2	3	4	5	6	7	8	9	10
....	1	2	3	4	5	6	7	8	9	10
....	1	2	3	4	5	6	7	8	9	10
....	1	2	3	4	5	6	7	8	9	10

Now collect feedback from one or more co-workers/colleagues and reflect on the discrepancies and similarities between the self-assessment and external assessment! If you don't have any co-workers or colleagues, ask someone you trust in your professional or private milieu to assess you!

The Authors

Marcello, Gianni and Jan Liscia (left to right)

Since its inception in 2000, taking shape in Paderborn, Germany, the name *Liscia Consulting* has gained ground on both national and international terrain with their excellent work in leader development. A most competent partner for strategy, conception and getting things done.

Business leaders Gianni, Marcello and Jan Liscia are not your everyday seminar conductors. Nor are they generic trainers or coaches. Gianni, Marcello and Jan Liscia are consultants who train and coach *leaders*. They are strategic partners, guiding and mediating transitional processes.

www.Liscia-Consulting.com

Keynote presentations for your event

On the pulse of change with inspiring keynote lectures! A keynote presentation can be designed to run 30 minutes or up to 3 hours – according to your event's agenda!

Together, we determine the focus of your D.R.E.A.M. of LEADERS® keynote lecture, i.e. Employee Engagement in Global Leadership, Transitional Process Leadership or Digital Leadership. Our multifarious and unusual approach infuses your business with new impulses, creating an atmosphere of awakening and a desire for change.

A rational/emotional composition coupled with the blunt, stark reality of our times invokes profound reflection. To easier digest discomfiting truth, we served it with a healthy portion of humor.

www.Liscia-Consulting.com

One 'n' Herman, the artist

Herman, illustrator

Herman is, and has been for some time, one of the most high-profile, successful pop art painters of our time. His edgy, idiosyncratic graphics and pictures are downright bodacious. Once a trained screen printer, his unleashed creativity has astonished viewers at over 200 national and international exhibits. Herman has been an independent artist since 1991.

Over the past years, the name Herman can also be found under cartoons drawn for a variety of German publishing houses. His *flying heart* comic strip in *Bravo*, a German youth magazine, was published several consecutive years, becoming a household name. The same can be said of the 18 Herman collector's glasses commissioned by *Ritzenhoff*. In 2007, bids were made for 49 Herman paintings at a charity auction benefiting the Peter Maffay Foundation.

www.Kuenstler-Herman.de

**Want more? Here's an overview of all books
by Gianni, Jan & Marcello Liscia:**

Gianni, Jan & Marcello Liscia

D.R.E.A.M.
of
LEADERS

Leadership is not an Illusion

Illustrations:
Herman Reichold

ISBN: 978-3-744-88271-2 – 19,90 € (D), E-Book: 14,99 € (D)

Gianni, Jan & Marcello Liscia

WORKBOOK
DEDICATION

Dedication to the work at hand, with heart and soul,
24 hours a day

Illustrations:
Herman Reichold

ISBN: 978-3-7528-5787-0 – 8,90 € (D), E-Book: 4,99 € (D)

Gianni, Jan & Marcello Liscia

WORKBOOK
RESPONSIBILITY

Showing responsibility for decisions made, for employees
and for oneself

Illustrations:
Herman Reichold

ISBN: 978-3-7528-5825-9 – 8,90 € (D), E-Book: 4,99 € (D)

Gianni, Jan & Marcello Liscia

WORKBOOK
ATTITUDE

A question of personal attitude and values which are
lived and experienced

Illustrations:
Herman Reichold

ISBN: 978-3-7528-5827-3 – 8,90 € (D), E-Book: 4,99 € (D)

Gianni, Jan & Marcello Liscia

WORKBOOK
MOTIVATION

Being ready to perform is the basis for all action

Illustrations:
Herman Reichold

ISBN: 978-3-7528-5828-0 – 8,90 € (D), E-Book: 4,99 € (D)

Gianni, Jan & Marcello Liscia

The Book of Happiness

A work and reflection diary

Illustrations:
Herman Reichold

ISBN: 978-3-7528-5829-7 – 8,90 € (D)

All of our titles are available as ebooks (except The Book of Happiness) and can be enjoyed in the German language, too!